THE HISTORY OF THE
WHITE HOUSE
COLORING BOOK

Steven James Petruccio

DOVER PUBLICATIONS, INC.
Mineola, New York

Note

This fascinating book about the history of the White House will take you from the very first American president, George Washington, to the administration of Barack Obama. Along the way, you'll learn some interesting facts—such as that the first president to live in the White House was not George Washington, but John Adams. You'll also find out how the White House got its name, why sheep grazed on the lawn, and when the first White House garden was planted. The building, which has undergone many changes over the years, remains an enduring symbol of President Washington's determination to build a home worthy of the new American government. Enjoy learning its history as you color the pages.

Bibliographical Note

The History of the White House Coloring Book is a new work, first published by
Dover Publications, Inc., in 2010.

International Standard Book Number

ISBN-13: 978-0-486-47556-1
ISBN-10: 0-486-47556-5

Manufactured in the United States by LSC Communications
47556504   2017
www.doverpublications.com

In 1790 President George Washington signed an Act of Congress declaring that the new home of the federal government would be located along the Potomac River. The site for the new residence was chosen by President Washington and Pierre L'Enfant, an artist and engineer. The city plan was laid out, with eighty-two acres reserved for a "President's Park." In 1791, the new "federal city" was named for George Washington.

On March 14, 1792, a competition was held for the design of a house for the president. James Hoban, an Irish-born architect, was selected for his pleasing design. In October 1792, the first cornerstone was laid and construction began of a mansion in the neo-classical Federal style, built of pale gray sandstone. President Washington oversaw the construction of the White House but never lived in it. When it was completed, the White House was five times smaller than originally planned, yet it was the largest house in the United States until the 1860s.

The White House was modeled after Leinster House in Ireland. The building had no **north or south porticos** [covered walkways with classical columns] in the original design. The **White House** was built by **both** free and enslaved African-Americans, European immigrants, and **Scottish stonemasons. The** south face of the structure, a bow-shaped center section modeled **after typical Irish country houses**, was originally planned as the main entrance.

The first president to live in the White House was John Adams. He arrived there on November 1, 1800. It was Adams who decided that the north side would be the main entrance to the new "President's House."

Although his furnishings and a portrait of George Washington were in place in his new home, many of the rooms were unfinished when President Adams and his family, who followed him one month later, moved in. They described the place as cold and damp, and tolerable as long as fires were lit in every room.

Construction of the White House was completed during the presidency of Thomas Jefferson. In 1806 Jefferson transformed the grand Entrance Hall into an art museum of sorts, displaying many artifacts brought to Washington by the Lewis and Clark expedition, including antlers, Native American costumes, and snake skins. During his presidency, Jefferson added two pavilions to the east and west portions of the residence to provide additional space.

Dolley Madison, the wife of President James Madison, played a major role in the social and political scenes in Washington, bringing together politicians, diplomats, and citizens at social gatherings. On the night of August 24, 1814, she and the president were to host a dinner for forty guests when they learned that the British had invaded Washington. The First Lady quickly moved to save valuable documents and silverware, as well as the full-length portrait of George Washington painted by Gilbert Stuart. The portrait is the only item from the interior of the original White House on display today.

During the War of 1812 between the United States and Britain, British troops marched into Washington on August 24, 1814, and proceeded to burn major government buildings. On August 25, they looted and set fire to the President's House, hoping to disgrace the president and the nation.

All that remained of the structure was the scorched exterior walls. There was talk of moving the nation's capital to a new location, but it was decided that the structure would be rebuilt—including the President's House—as a sign of unity and victory.

James Hoban, along with Benjamin Henry Latrobe, a British-born American architect, was called upon to oversee the reconstruction of the President's House, which lasted from 1815 until 1817. The new sandstone structure was given a coat of white paint to cover scorch marks. Prior to this, the stone had been sealed with a coating of whitewash made of lime, rice glue, casein, and lead to protect it from the elements. Thus, it was commonly referred to as the White House. The name was formalized by President Theodore Roosevelt.

In October 1817, President James Monroe moved into the rebuilt house. It was still unfinished on the inside, but Monroe was determined to have it completed in order to receive visitors on January 1—a tradition begun during the presidency of Thomas Jefferson. Monroe purchased furnishings for the rooms and opened the house to the public, as planned.

In 1824 James Hoban was brought back to supervise the building of a south portico on the White House, which he had planned to do prior to 1814.

The architect Benjamin Latrobe drew the plans for south and north porticos. Vertical columns were added, as well as a porch with a double set of stairs leading up to it.

In 1829 President Andrew Jackson secured the funds to build the North Portico. James Hoban was again brought in to oversee its construction. The portico covered the driveway to serve as a carriage entrance. Decorative roses similar to those of the previous structure were carved near the columns to link the portico to the older doorway.

President James Polk placed a statue of Thomas Jefferson in the center of the north lawn of the White House in 1848. Seasonal flowers were planted around the statue. This new garden, separated from the residence by an iron fence, was open to the public every day.

In 1857 President James Buchanan built a wooden greenhouse on the roof of the west terrace. In later years the original structure was replaced by glass-and-iron greenhouses, and additional conservatories, including rose and orchid houses, were added. Filled with plants and flowers, they became a favorite location of many First Ladies.

The South Lawn of the White House once was a wide, open meadow leading to a marsh. Over the years it was filled in and graded to create a large circular lawn, known as the "President's Park." In 1875, during the presidency of Ulysses S. Grant, the first fountain was installed. Frederick Law Olmstead designed the South Lawn as it exists today, with specimen plantings and private areas for the First Family, as well as public views of the residence.

The conservatories were torn down in 1902 and room was made to add a new West Wing to the White House. President Theodore Roosevelt found that there was not enough space in the residence for his large family, as well as his staff. The new building would house the official staff offices. The structure had a central office for the president, which was remodeled in 1909 to include the first Oval Office.

During World War I, President Woodrow Wilson brought sheep to the White House to graze on the South Lawn; these animals would save manpower and money needed to mow the lawn. In addition, the wool sheared from the sheep would be sold to raise funds for the Red Cross. The sheep remained on the grounds until 1920.

The first White House garden was planted in 1825 by John Quincy Adams and his gardener,
John Housely. A small colonial garden was established in 1902 by Edith Roosevelt, Theodore
Roosevelt's wife.

This garden was intended to replace the rose conservatory that had stood in its place. (In 1961, during the Kennedy administration, the garden was redesigned by Rachel Lambert Mellon; it featured a large central lawn with flower beds, bordered by trees. The beds are planted with grandiflora and tea roses. Seasonal flowers such as tulips and chrysanthemums are planted to add year-round color.) The modern-day garden is pictured here.

In 1927, structural problems were discovered in the roof of the White House. The roof was replaced and the attic converted into a third story to accommodate guests and service rooms. Later, a sunroom was added by First Lady Grace Coolidge on the site of the present-day solarium.

In 1934, as part of the WPA (Works Progress Administration), President Franklin D. Roosevelt had the West Wing expanded to house more offices. A second story was built and the basement was enlarged. The Oval Office was moved to its present location in the southeast corner to give the president more privacy and to overlook the Rose Garden.

In 1942, the glass-enclosed wing originally built in 1902 on the east side of the White House was torn down; it had served as an entrance for social functions and had deteriorated over the years. A new East Wing was constructed featuring a formal entrance, offices, and an underground fallout shelter.

In 1948, President Harry S. Truman requested that a second-floor balcony be built in order to provide shade for the first floor, where the awnings were continually soiled and needed replacing. The new balcony, built by architect Lorenzo S. Winslow, was an improvement to the appearance and functioning of the White House.

While building the Truman balcony, Winslow conducted a structural survey of the White House and found that it was being stressed to its limit due to the weight of the third-floor construction.

The survey found cracks in many walls. The Commission on the Renovation of the Executive Mansion decided to retain the exterior walls of the residence; the interior would be removed and reassembled on a new skeleton of steel beams. A new concrete foundation was to be poured as well. In the end, little of the original interior remained, although attempts were made to recreate the look and feel of the original rooms. This reconstruction was completed in 1952.

Remodeling of the White House Press Briefing Room began in 2005. This room sits atop an indoor swimming pool that had been built for President Franklin D. Roosevelt. (The pool area now houses press operations wiring.) The original room was constructed in 1969 to accommodate the increasing number of White House news reporters; it was renamed the James S. Brady Press Briefing Room in 2000 for President Ronald Reagan's press secretary. The room was renovated and reopened in 2007.

To address increasing worldwide environmental awareness and the need for healthier eating habits, First Lady Michelle Obama decided to plant a vegetable garden. The White House Kitchen Garden is the first vegetable garden on the White House grounds since Eleanor Roosevelt's wartime Victory Garden. A site was selected on the South Lawn and ground was broken for the garden, which was planted to yield lettuce, spinach, collards, berries, and herbs.

With attention being paid to the historic significance of the residence's interior and exterior, the White House stands today as a symbol of the United States that is recognized throughout the world. In 2000, a reenactment of the arrival of President John Adams took place to commemorate the two-hundredth anniversary of the White House.